BOBBETT, HOOPER & CO., N. Y.

RIP VAN WINKLE

AND

HIS WONDERFUL NAP.

BY

EDMUND CLARENCE STEDMAN.

WITH ILLUSTRATIONS BY SOL. EYTINGE, JR.,

ENGRAVED AND PRINTED IN COLORS BY BOBBETT, HOOPER, & CO.

BOSTON:
FIELDS, OSGOOD, & CO.
1870.

WELCH,
BIGELOW,
& CO.
UNIVERSITY
PRESS.

RIP VAN WINKLE.

THIS way, children, and hear me tell
Of Rip Van Winkle's wonderful nap, —
The oddest fortune that ever befell
A merry and good-for-nothing chap ;
Of all the snoozes and slumbers deep,
The strangest, longest, and strongest sleep !
Up in the heart of the Hudson hills,
The lordly, beautiful Kaaterskills.

Who has not heard of the Catskill peaks,
Lifting their haunted tops so high
From the deep, broad vale, which the river seeks,
To the thunder-clouds in the summer sky ?
Their sides are red in the morning sun,
And blue and golden when day is done,
But in misty Autumn you see them stand
In all the colors of Fairyland.

Under these mountains snuggling down,
In Sixteen Hundred and Sixty-Six,
The Dutchmen were building Kaatskill town
Of crockery-ware and Holland bricks ;
There were lots of windmills and weather-vanes,
The gable-windows had latticed panes,
And every house had a sanded floor,
With a cabbage-garden before the door.

It was *yah Mynheer*, and *yah ya Vrouw ;*
The goodwives spun in the open air ;
The men wore breeches, as records show,
Ten kinds at a time, pair over pair ;
They looked all day at the weathercock
And smoked their pipes, but at eight o'clock
They drank some schnapps, and wagged their heads
And covered themselves with feather-beds.

In Seventeen Hundred and Sixty-Six,
When we were under King George the Third,
The queer old people began to mix
Their Dutch and their English, word for word ;
But in gartered hose they stumped about,
And lived on bacon and pickled kraut,
While a burgomaster ruled the town
And the children feared his terrible frown !

Rip Van Winkle, who farmed it here,
With his son and daughter and scolding wife,
Whenever the latter was n't near
Led a jolly and harum-scarum life.
Dunder ! how he would idle and shirk,
Wet weather or dry, his regular work !
His roof was leaky, his larder bare,
And his buckskin breeches let in the air.

Little for this cared easy Rip,
As he roamed the hills for squirrels and quail,
With a game-pouch dangling over his hip,
And Wolf, his dog, at a moment's hail;
But when from the woods he sauntered down,
And they saw him idling through the town,
Blitzen! how the children would run
To Rip Van Winkle, and then what fun!

They mounted his back and pulled at his leg;
He made their whistles and flew their kites,
Or played at marbles and mumble-the-peg,
Or told them stories of Indian fights.
There was n't a dog in Kaatskill street
But knew him and ran between his feet;
His little son Rip was lazy as he,
And both were thoughtless as well could be.

So Dame Van Winkle's merciless tongue
Berated them every day and night,
For a pair of idlers, old and young, —
She fairly drove them out of her sight!
Even Wolf, the dog, when he heard her speak,
Would drop his tail with a sidelong sneak,
And all three together would make retreat
To King George's Inn at head of the street.

Then Dame Van Winkle would tell her wrongs
To every gossip who chanced within,
While Rip was smoking and singing songs
On the wooden bench in front of the inn:
He and his cronies three together, —
Derrick Van Bummel, clerk of the weather,
Brom Dutcher, a graceless wight and bold,
And Nicholas Vedder, the landlord old.

One day, when the hills were full of game,
And the autumn woods were crimson bright,
Rip stole away from his work and Dame,
And hunted far up the mountain height;
Till at last he sat him down to rest
Where the eagle builds his lofty nest,
And looked below at the landscape wide
And the silvery Hudson's distant tide.

Behind, a craggy and dismal glen,
Like a worn-out crater, fell aslant.
Rip saw that the sun was setting then,
And time to get home was growing scant.
He whistled his dog, and "Wolf," said he,
"'T is a dog's life truly for you and me!
Let 's home, or you 'll get a broken pate,
And lose your supper for staying late!"

Just as the words had crossed his lip,
Some neighboring voice the truant heard
Cry — "Rip Van Winkle! Van Winkle! RIP!"
Like Robinson Crusoe's famous bird.
"RIP VAN WINKLE!" it piped again.
Rip looked above and beneath in vain;
"I 'm sure," he said, "that I heard a call!"
And he felt his flesh begin to crawl.

The dog slunk close to his master's knee,
And gave a growl, and bristled his hair,
But into the glen peered wistfully,
Till the huntsman's glances followed there
And saw a stranger climbing alone,
With a burden over his shoulder thrown;
And Rip, though puzzled and half afraid,
Went down to proffer his ready aid.

Bobbett & Hooper N.Y.

Greater still were his wonder and fear
  When he marked the grave, outlandish mien
Of the stranger, as they drew more near.
  The doublet he wore was linsey-green,
His baggy breeches were short and wide,
With rows of buttons on either side;
His figure was squat and his visage square,
And grizzle-gray were his beard and hair.

A peak'd hat covered his bushy head,
  And his shoulder carried a liquor-keg;
Never a Christian word he said,
  But he beckoned, as if to say — "I beg
You will somewhat lighten me of my load
Along this rather uncertain road!"
So each in his turn the runlet bore,
And the stranger silently went before.

Over the rocks and brush he led,
  Till they clambered up a steep ravine,
Where an ancient torrent had left its bed,
  And the fronting cliffs were dark between;
From the gloomy fissure there came a sound
Of thunder rumbling along the ground!
Rip halted a little, but quickly thought,
"'T is some passing storm in the highlands caught."

So on he followed, and passed the cleft,
  And reached a hollow that opened wide,
A mountain-chamber the giants left
  When they split the peaks from side to side;
Tall cliffs encircled it with their wall,
And the twilight glimmered over it all;
And there on the level, as Rip could see,
Was gathered a wondrous companie.

They seemed a strange, seafaring band,
  Some forty swaggerers, wearing the dress
Of an olden time or foreign land;
  Whence they had come, Rip could not guess;
Some were covered like Punchinello
In sugar-loaf hats and jerkins yellow,
And they wore long knives, and breeches wide,
Like those of the grim and solemn guide.

One was a Captain over the rest,
  With steeple-hat and cockerel feather,
A gold-laced doublet about his breast,
  And high-heeled shoes of Flemish leather.
Thought Rip to himself, "One never knew
Such a lonely, drear, fantastic crew!
I almost wish I were safe and sound
With Dame Van Winkle on lower ground!"

How do you think their time was spent?
  Playing at ninepins, like sailors bold.
And just as oft as a ball was sent,
  That noise of thunder rattled and rolled
Along the mountain from crag to crag!
Rip felt his courage begin to flag;
For night had come, and he saw in the skies
The stars were busily winking their eyes.

Suddenly then those bowlers grim
  Gathered about and ceased their play,
But all were speechless and stared at him
  In a ghastly, mystical sort of way.
His comrade emptied the spirits out
In flagons for Rip to serve about;
Then silently drank they all, and deep,
And wiped their beards with a stately sweep.

The magical liquor bubbled and hissed,
And a pungent savor of Hollands rose,
Which no Van Winkle could ever resist
When under a true Van Winkle's nose.
Rip ventured to sip it upon the sly, —
His legs were tired and his lips were dry;
He gained Dutch courage each time he quaffed,
Till he winked at the Captain, and loudly laughed.

Then loudly laughed the motley crew,
And furious balls they swiftly bowled,
And far and wide the ninepins flew,
And loud the thunder rattled and rolled,
Till players and rocks and trees and skies
Went whirling around before Rip's eyes,
And there in that mountain chasm deep,
As midnight fell, — he fell into a SLEEP!

When he woke, the birds were singing around,
The sun was bright in the morning-tide,
And he found himself on the spot of ground
Whence first he followed his stranger guide.
"Hallo!" he said, "have I slept all night
So far from home, on this lonesome height?
That terrible flagon was much to blame!
What kind of a tale shall I tell the Dame?"

An old, old gun, with its stock all punk,
Its barrel all rust, beside him lay:
"I see! those pirates have made me drunk
And taken my dog and gun away!"
They had played him a scurvy trick, 't was plain:
"Where 's Wolf? Here, Wolf!" But he whistled in vain,
And the cries of a passing flock of crows
Seemed to laugh at his groanings as he rose.

"O dear! my elbows and knees are sore;
My back is lame with the rheumatiz!
I 'll lie out-doors in the dew no more!
'T will lay me up for a week, as it is.
Dunder! I 'm famished for want of food;
This sleep on the mountain brings no good;
If my poor stiff legs will carry me down,
Just catch me again so far from town!"

Through birch and hazel and sassafras
He stumbled homewards, well as he could,
With many a halt to mutter, "Alas,
This night on the mountain has brought no good!"
As he neared the village, by mid of day,
The people he met along the way
Seemed strangers and oddly dressed: "I ought
To know every one hereabouts," he thought.

All stopped, and noticed him with surprise,
Till he looked where he saw their glances rest,
And found that his beard (could he trust his eyes?)
Had grown so long it covered his breast,
Mildewed, tangled, rusty and gray!
"Who 's that old hermit?" he heard them say:
So queer the village and people seemed,
He pinched himself to see if he dreamed.

The streets he entered were altered, too,
All upside down and shifted about,
And full of houses he never knew.
Shaking his head, he said "No doubt
That draught of Hollands has made this change
In my fuddled brain, — but 't is very strange!"
And wandered along a central road
Till at length he found his own abode.

Alack! the rafters had fallen in,
  The door was broken, the rooms were bare;
A dog like Wolf was skulking within,
  But neither the wife nor children were there.
"Dame! Judith! Rip!" The mouldering walls
Gave a dismal echo to his calls,
And the cur ran growling out of view:
"My dog," he muttered, "forsakes me, too!"

When out in the street he stood once more
  Strange children jeered wherever he came,
Strange dogs were barking from every store,
  Each sign-board flaunted an unknown name.
So towards the Inn he made, with a pack
Of boys and women behind his back.
Alas! when he reached the wonted place
What mystery stared him in the face?

"The Union Hotel" stood on the site
  Which the old stone Tavern held of yore,
'T was a wooden building painted white,
  With a liberty-pole anigh the door.
And where King George, with his face benign,
Still looked both ways from the swinging sign,
They had painted a soldier's trappings on,
And labelled him "General Washington."

A crowd of people was there in front,
  A lean, long-featured, talkative throng.
Rip saw not one of the gossips wont
  To lounge and smoke with him all day long,
But caught such words of a loud oration
As "Congress," "Freedom," "this glorious Nation,"
And heard the farmers about him say
It was fairish weather for 'Lection Day.

My! how they jibed at his beard and hair,
  And flouted his ragged, mildewed coat!
The orator saw him standing there,
  And paused to ask him how he would vote,
And whether he entered their peace and quiet,
With a mob at his heels, to breed a riot?
Rip paled at the thought of such a thing,
And said he was loyal to the King.

"A tory!" they shouted, — "a British spy!"
  "Look out for his weapon!" "Seize his arm!"
"Let 's give him his fill of royalty!"
  Rip faltered out that he meant no harm,
He once had friends in the neighborhood,
And would like to hear of them, if he could.
"Well, tell us their names, old fellow," they said,
"You seem to have risen from the dead."

"Where 's Landlord Vedder?" "His grave is filled,"
  Said a little old man, "these eighteen years!"
"Brom Dutcher?" "At Stony Point was killed."
  "Van Bummel, then?" "O, he, it appears,
Is a member of Congress, famous grown."
Rip sickened to find himself alone,
His house a ruin, his friends gone past:
"Where 's Rip Van Winkle?" he said at last.

"Van Winkle? Yonder, the lazy elf,
  Smoking his pipe beneath that tree."
Rip saw with wonder his very self,
  Or another like him as like could be;
"That 's me, indeed, — that 's Rip! 't is true!
I 'm not myself, and all is so new, —
Last night I slept on the mountain, — and now
I 'm changed, and my dog is gone, and my vrouw!"

"Rip, the old man won't hurt you, dear!"
  Said a mother who led her child that way.
The wanderer turned as it caught his ear:
  "Kind woman, what is your name, I pray?"
"Judith." His eyes began to twinkle; [Winkle.
"And your father's?" "His name was Rip Van
One time — 't was twenty years since, alack!
He went a hunting, and never came back."

"And where 's your mother?" he asked at length.
  "She died in a bleeding-fit, last year,
Scolding a peddler beyond her strength,
  Just after I married Gardenier."
"One change for the better among the rest!"
Thought Rip, and he caught her to his breast.
"Judith! I am your father!" he cried,
"Lost all this time on the mountain side.

"And there 's my son, — and it makes me weep,
  For only last night, it seems to me,
He was small as your's — and I went to sleep —
  Now I 'm old, and I don't know how it can be.
And your husband, — he 's one of the little boys
Who sat and watched me making their toys.
Does nobody, then, in all this crowd,
Know Rip Van Winkle?" he sobbed aloud.

"I used to know him," said one old dame,
  "When he went away he was in his prime;
Why, yes! 't is himself, the very same!
  Sho! where have you travelled all this time?"

Rip told his tale to the crowd about,
But they shook their heads with prudent doubt,
Till Peter Vanderdonk came along,
The sage and counsellor of the throng.

He vouched for Rip, and declared he knew,
  From a wise tradition handed down,
That Sir Hendrick Hudson and his crew
  Still haunted the mountain near the town;
Each twentieth year they gathered there;
Whoever should meet with them, and dare
To drink of their flagon, would slumber then
Till the twentieth year came round again.

Rip lived in peace at his daughter's home,
  And trotted his grandchild on his knee,
Nor after that was he known to roam,
  But smoked his pipe, a widower free.
With an old man's right, he sat once more
On the bench in front of the tavern door,
And told his tale, as I tell it to-day,
To every stranger who passed that way.

And still, when the Autumn days are warm,
  Though fourscore years have speeded by,
You can hear a sound like a thunder-storm
  Pass over those mountain summits high;
You can hear the echoes rattle and roll
With every ball that the Dutchmen bowl,
Far up in the heart of the Hudson hills,
The lordly, beautiful Kaaterskills.

BOBBETT, HOOPER & CO., N. Y.

www.ingramcontent.com/pod-product-compliance
Lightning Source LLC
LaVergne TN
LVHW020643110826
845149LV00004B/1332

* 9 7 8 1 4 1 8 1 8 9 8 8 4 *